A
Lioness
at my
Heels

A Lioness at my Heels

Robin Winckel-Mellish

P O Box 385, Athlone, 7760, South Africa
modjaji.books@gmail.com
http://modjaji.book.co.za

ISBN 978-1-920397-43-2

Book design: Natascha Mostert
Cover artwork and lettering: Jesse Breytenbach
Printed and bound by Mega Digital, Cape Town
Set in Palatino

Acknowledgements:
Some of these poems have been published by:
DVoice and *Versal* (Amsterdam), SAND (Berlin).
Special thanks to Colleen Higgs and Angela
Voges for their interest and encouragement.

For Kate Foley and the poets of Amsterdam
who have shown me the way of words.

Contents

One

Two

Three

One

The leaf-rakers

Out of nowhere they appear,
women the colour of autumn,
scraping the heels of moon-hills,
sweeping the bones of borders

as if sleepwalking.
Kraal women raking dust,
loose as water, rippling vessels
of clay and sepia, swathed infants

bundled on their backs.
Slack as cobras, broken shadow
is transmuted on paths
and pools and garden walls

earth bodies. And I in silk gown
breakfast on mango and papaya
as crackling twig brooms herd
the bonanza spilled all around.

Tulips

Losing all notion of time.
　　Trying to remember, wondering

whether you are still there, or just
　　looking in from the periphery.

When you took the simple wooden table,
　　peanut porridge and the leather

fertility bracelet with you to Paris,
　　when tulips on the balcony

refused to grow, when hemispheres
　　were crossed with letters, like sharp

swallows diving with the smell of rain.
　　An open jar of ancient honey.

Family

My grandfather had a secret longing for fish. Silver scales and a tail instead of legs. He said he gaffed a mermaid, pulled barnacles from her teeth, her breath smelled of redbait. My grandmother would sourly sit knitting. The sharp click of her needles would stitch a bolero for the naked mermaid. My grandfather always told *so* many stories.

My father lived in a wooden shack on a wild shore amongst the baboons, rock rabbits and a leopard. He caught fish and ran water from the high waterfall into the valley. His bath was hot at midday, cold in the morning. His evenings were candlelit and he noticed that when he had drunk brandy, a slinky lynx would wink at him through the window.

My brother fell in love with a Koi fish. She ate from his hand, her soft mouth nuzzling his fingers, her cold body touching his outstretched hands. He sat for hours watching her under the stars, darting here and there she was never far from him. Now she has spawned a whole school of Koi and he has built a bigger pond for her, larger than his house. The pool is growing, my brother is poor. But he is happy.

Ring

That I was lost three times says
more about you than me. You

tell the story in amazement
how I kept turning up. Once

like a tortoise without its shell,
the diamond had fallen out.

Now I'm reset, reinvented
on your knuckled finger

safer now that your hand is thicker,
your hair as ashen as my pale glitter.

A small southern star
you let me go, dropped me

in a cabbage patch, and each time
I came back. I wonder why

pure and clear as a child's eyes
you let me slip.

A cup of words
(inspired by Billy Collins)

People ring us up about words,
spelling, or a meaning
the Dutch want answers quickly.
We tell them gently coax the sentence
like you would a bird, or a wild cat.
But all they want is to torture
the sense out of it, beat it with a stick,
spin it around while trying
to find a sensible translation.

Hold a cup of words to the ear,
each wave pushes and pulls
resonates the tide coming in
as the sea soothes its song.
Play them a little, see how they sound,
unravel them gently then let them go.

Het hoort erbij
(It's all part of it)

Walking the beach is a game.
Sand sculptures like discovered poems:
a clenched fist, a giant crab,
a heart decorated in shells,
one long wave and all is flattened.
They say *het hoort erbij*.

A young boy sweeping the storm's
sand from the deck, shucked carpets
of molluscs and carapace,
happy in the lurching wind saying
that by tomorrow it will have blown in again,
het hoort erbij.

The caretaker

She arrived when Father was ailing,
her dark hair a shining shield,
the grey curl a dove's wing

fluttering on her forehead.
She took him in hand,
soothed, rearranged, his high cot

looked onto the rose garden.
She washed him mornings,
his mouth puckered in a lewd smile,

jackal eyes peered down at her hands,
his grey skin gleamed,
in the warm rush of water.

Father was hers, his faltering step
his feeble mind, the white towel
loose around his hips.

Eventually being

Fashion is about eventually being naked
 — Vivienne Westwood

It begins with a puff. In dimness my eye
is tricked into thinking your silken curled
scarf is an adder, instead it's a tie.
I follow the zigzag trail. The blurred
bits and pieces, shades of peacock,
odd socks, all droppings, disturbed.
And on the floor like a stumbling block,
a pair of grey trousers, elegant, reserved.
And tiptoeing closer I can sense your form,
a doorway leading to the deeper reach.
Though I can't see, I know your skin is warm
like smooth slivers on hot milk. And through each
opening a wildebeest is roaring, tusks glinting
in moonlight, grunting and snoring.

The baker

What I suspected is true. I tasted the cake. The baker says it is best eaten on special occasions. He cut off the tip of his finger while chopping apples and embarrassed kept the finger bandaged for weeks, frightened that the women would turn away when they noticed what was missing. Now he lights candles, kindles the fire. In this nutmeg cave of the bakery the ovens are heating. Heaps of flour fold like bulging thighs. Cherries are set out for decoration, the pea-sized butter pearls have been weighed. First he breaks an egg with one hand, switches to the other so that both hands become evenly strong and as sensitive as a mandolin player's. Now he can break two eggs. Sometimes he requires dozens of eggs. He looks away so that he can develop his sense of touch. He says he cannot stop the feeling and must follow. He says that when the sun is severed from the sky, light shines through fingers of moon. The hands knead, the mix quickens.

Ceremony

The bride has arrived to welcome guests, finely
packaged in crimson silk, tiny feet, cinnabar lips.

The mother of the bride takes the daughter's hand,
a crushed lucky envelope, presses it into mine, gives her

tells her be obedient. Are not ourselves most
precious of gifts, marriages measured

in delicate balance, as warm water poured
over tea. Chrysanthemum, lily, rose,

the rhythmic stirring of leaves, signifying
the three nods of the Phoenix.

Look at the tea in appreciation
she says, before you taste.

I have received the gift of the mother-in-law.
In the cup of glass, green leaves sink

waves of water release fragrance.

Anniversary eggs

Poached eggs will change our lives.
Like clouds taking on rounded shapes

bubbling in boiling nests,
they form creamy bundles

symbols of content,
rite of passage into golden years.

Always scrambled or very often fried, poached
seem enticing, think of Eggs Benedict!

Sunday brunch will be sumptuous now
served on the old silver tray in the morning sun.

So that's what you got for your wedding anniversary.
an elegant poaching pan with four heart ramekins

that coddle eggs. But then the Hollandaise.
Believed to mimic a Dutch sauce, it needs

to be beaten to hold its shape, if not
the eggs will separate in an oily mess.

Nothing more attractive than a man
who revels in the creative experience, *you*

must prepare it. The difficulty is making
the emulsification hold fast, fear of botching it,

the thought of whipping so long that wrists ache,
having to get it right the old-fashioned way

with no cheating. Half a spoon of flour,
a pinch of arrowroot is enough subterfuge,

the buttercup sauce lies stiff
as salted herring on the toasted bed.

Tw

Walking the lioness

I'm a lioness slouching
down the *Hooftstraat*
on a diamond-studded leash.

Man-eater, alter ego, alley cat,
I'm spooked by a naked gaze,
those fur-draped shoulder blades.

I'm having a hard time keeping up,
feeling my cat breath taut –
shivering inside my skin

I'll make the break,
follow a bush-scent back
into wilderness. Loose now

on the run, I'll sink teeth
into knucklebone, spill
sapphires from my mouth.

Seven glasses of red wine

each day is what it takes
to desilt our bodies, rid us
of toxins says the woman
next to me, taking a sip
as she explains all that goes
into making a wonderful
new medication made from the skins
of the life-giving grape.
David Attenborough is in the Kalahari,
a tiny San woman is eating roots and tubers
and the meat of a Kudu her man
has spent all day tracking,
her low-lipid body taut and wiry.
Everything that is taken meets the needs,
and is not more than required.
Pamela, draped in sparkles
sips to get the stream pulsing
along her opening channels,
up to the smallest tributaries,
a flood of goodness
in the murky delta of river.

Kalahari Blue

Here there is nothing but Camel Thorn trees. Crumpled shadows
enfold the low scrub, then the rural dwellings and chicken coops,
a pale shell in an ocean of bushveld. The day's heat subsides and
the sisters welcome the gloam, a visible spectrum between green
and indigo. In the house the music player is turned on and the
microphone connected. Outside the night sky begins its glitter,
fireflies have reached the Milky Way. Two frail sisters put on frocks,
carefully comb hair. They will sing the one song they are good at,
the only song they remember: *Blue on blue, heartache on heartache* ...
As if tracking a Kudu they spear memory into music. Bruised shades
of melody lift, as if a sea of driftwood is rolling. Turning, pushing
forward, pulling back. The karaoke sounds grow louder, the cadence
heavier. Somewhere in the shadow a hyena is laughing. Whoops as
she brings down an antelope, sings as she tears the flesh, finds the
chamber of its heart. Drags the carcass to her den like a sack of love.

The same language

We had flown the midriff of the world to sit outside and stars were appearing low, as if eavesdropping. Food, friends and a balmy atmosphere set sentiment free, words hung ripe as the day let go, slipping quickly into dusk. Farm dogs barked and music drifted off into the vineyards. Conversation took a new direction, and, hungry for answers I needed to probe: *Why did you return?* At first he shrugged it off, rose to pour another glass of Chardonnay, an ibis flew up into the oak. Later he said he'd thought about it, had come to the conclusion it was about speaking the same language. *Can you imagine,* he said, *what it would be like not to speak the same language as your own children?* I shivered. Had I been oblivious to mine?

Old Rose

I remember her shuffling silver-slippered
from her kitchen burrow only once.
A rare outdoor show under the giant
umbrella palm, porcupine eyes watering
in green light, a child's birthday cake
held alight as she jived to *Rock around the clock.*

She snoozed in a musty hole beside
the ironing room, tired bed propped
up on four bricks to keep away evil spirits,
acrid smell of cigarette smoke,
rotting geraniums on the windowsill.

Old Rose was roast chicken on Sunday,
golden fishcakes stiff with parsley,
warm pumpkin fritters laced with cinnamon.
Bloated packages of bosom and bottom
stuffed into a starched white uniform.

Madiba*

As a boy he would take ash,
rub the tuft above his forehead,
in imitation of his Zulu father,
a country boy with four mothers
barefoot in cone-shaped huts.

So long he has lived,
his white peppercorn curls
now snug as a halo returned
to the land of the Thembu tribe.

Like a snake swallowing its tail
he holds a curl of circle,
her handwriting, the birthday envelope
falls like a bird from his slingshot.

He first felt her darkness when just
a ploughboy, she showed him
his fangs, her wildcat words
now spilling over his fingers.

He knows, everything she is
is him, her aliveness buried
in the dimpled hills of his skin,
cracks and crevices where freedom
made a hero out of a herdsman.

* Madiba is Nelson Mandela

Warrior

Baas, Madam, anyone at home?
He has planted himself outside my yard
like a tough-hard Kalahari tree.
No bling bling, no shining thing, no money.

Mantis hands reach up, pod fingers
dangle through the fence, barbed
scar running from nose to ear.

I listen to his tales: yesterday his wife,
today his mother,
pass coins through the ironwork

and as the tiny silver moons
of his face light up,
a blazing smile bursts open.

Crickets

They have their hours.

Just before dawn when a watery
light creeps in they are furious,
and then curiously quiet until the sun is high.
At midday, and again in evening they rub
their spidery legs in passionate pleas.

They are a seething mass, everywhere.

Under twigs and driftwood they rampage
in hordes, legs, heads, eyes, fluttering wings,
flying, crawling, chirping, copulating,
stiff-legged little bastards, dizzy
with their own noise, frantic to tell
the world how important they are.

Cloud cats

The heavens are on safari.
By late afternoon lions leap the sky,
the atmospheric pressure is rising.

Cat-clouds are slouching apparitions,
drift together, lick each other,
lash out as the breeze accelerates.

A lioness has gone hunting,
her creamy silhouette bounds along.
A black beard has lost his mane

and further on some thunder-cloud
cubs are playing roll over,
rumble, tumble.

I'm flat on my back in the grass
cat-napping, your mouth
presses a kiss like a roar.

Restaurant Mozambique

We are hungry, not for the taste
of each other but the sting
of peri-peri, so we veer off
the highway. A white gate,
cattle grid, half-planted wine bottles
protect the aloe beds, the tin-roofed
shack shimmering in sunset,
porcupine-quill lampshades
and the intimacy of Casa do Sol.
Smells of garlic and prawns,
the grit of sand at the back
of our teeth, I close my eyes

and freefall, already stone drunk
before we have even ordered.

The voodoo of spoons

After the third I knew it was more
than just the thought of you holding
the ivory handle, or eating
from an ebony paw that enticed me

to pick them up in steamy bazaars
and pass them on to you.
A wild sense had taken root
in my voodoo soil,

spirits had been sent to stir me,
egged me on to buy the tiny silver one,
the elephant spoon, and the calabash ladle
large enough for two.

In a sun-drugged world of witchdoctors,
where animal bones are thrown for prophecy
and bowls of samp offered to the dead,
your image dances.

Vanishing point

Like the hovering wings of a sea eagle,
the slender threads of spider web,
our collar bones could be guitar strings,
our pelvic shells an abstract work of art.

At night, on the moon, we superglue
our hands and feet our nipples and lips
and become a single vanishing point.

We elephant-dance, caress the neat creases,
so we don't know where one begins
and the other ends, my love.

Like night music, or a love-drunk vibration,
an experiment gone awry,
I've got us mixed up.

Three

Meditation while waiting for something unpleasant

If my mind wanders
it's to that stone farmhouse
beside the winding dust road,
the ostriches, a few palms,
a creaky bridge over a dried-up stream.
What is the point of remembering
that curve of road,
that hamlet, without one
touch of green?
A passing bakkie churns
up a barrow of dust,
then the limitless silence.

And when it happens,
like a pigeon crazed for home
I'm racing back,
dark clouds pass,
the light dry road opens.

Paper boat

I could have thrown
    all to the wind. Forgotten

the sleepless night
    my foxy odour

mud on the kitchen floor.
    Instead, when you pull

me down, I'm holding myself
    a paper boat on a roaring pond

set to yield by the spillway.

What I want is to say: *Look here*
    knees, breasts, *let go.*

Home

Tea-cups pile to the edge
of the draining board like wildebeest
in desperate rows, jumping
the dishwater at its narrowest point.
Newly-washed shirts dry in the sun
spread out like giant termites.
Yesterday's ironing blooms,
a flowering cactus
after a moist day's heat.
Cool beds in the morning unmade
and unruly, white horses on Zeekoevlei,*
Africa follows me around the house
a lioness at my heels.

* Hippopotamus Lake

Around four

It's probably around four.
No sounds yet of birdsong, little light,
just an early driver, a delivery, something.

Dog's bark, short, sharp. No wind, oyster-still.
Navigating the fringes, forgotten half-faces.
They will be out, others rising, the sun

positioned somewhere. Body shapes
hollow the clouds of sheet,
the mechanics of breath knitted in sleep.

Other titles by Hands-On Books

Lava Lamp Poems
by Colleen Higgs

Difficult to Explain
edited by Finuala Dowling

Looking for Trouble
by Colleen Higgs